SCIENCE BUDDIES

30-MINUTE ROBOTICS PROJECTS

Loren Bailey

Lerner Publications ◆ Minneapolis

Science Buddies is a registered trademark of Science Buddies and used under license. Copyright © 2019 Science Buddies, Milpitas, CA 95035

Official Licensed Product
Lerner Publications Company
A division of Lerner Publishing Group, Inc.
241 First Avenue North
Minneapolis, MN 55401 USA

For reading levels and more information, look up this title at www.lernerbooks.com.

Main body text set in Hoosker Don't.
Typeface provided by The Chank Company.

Library of Congress Cataloging-in-Publication Data

Names: Bailey, Loren, author.
Title: 30-minute robotics projects / by Loren Bailey.
Other titles: Thirty minute robotics projects
Description: Minneapolis : Lerner Publications, [2019] | Series: 30-minute makers | Includes bibliographical references and index. | Audience: Ages 7–11. | Audience: Grades 4 to 6.
Identifiers: LCCN 2018011187 (print) | LCCN 2018019841 (ebook) | ISBN 9781541542877 (eb pdf) | ISBN 9781541538887 (lb : alk. paper)
Subjects: LCSH: Robotics—Juvenile literature.
Classification: LCC TJ211.2 (ebook) | LCC TJ211.2 .B353 2019 (print) | DDC 629.8/92—dc23

LC record available at https://lccn.loc.gov/2018011187

Manufactured in the United States of America
1-45071-35898-10/11/2018

CONTENTS

For more information on
materials kits and even
more free robotics projects,
scan this QR code!

LET'S GET BUILDING!

Beep berp! Do you love robots? Did you know you can create your own robot in thirty minutes or less?

Science is all about tinkering, exploring, and learning from experience. So let's get ready to experiment!

After you've finished a project, add your own spin to it. What kind of robot will you create next?

BEFORE YOU GET STARTED

Stay safe! When working on projects that use exposed wires, do not let the red and black wires touch. This would create a short circuit and drain the battery. Some projects require sharp tools or hot objects. Ask an adult's permission before using them. Keep your workspace clear, and protect it with newspaper or cardboard. This makes cleanup easy too!

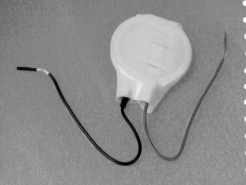

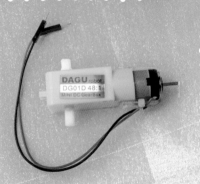

Gather your materials ahead of time. You can find materials for these projects online or in a hardware store. If you have trouble finding materials, visit Science Buddies online for more information. Some projects may require stripping the insulation off wire if not enough metal is exposed. Ask an adult for help using a wire stripper.

PROGRAMMING MAZE

Computer programs tell robots what to do and how to move. Write a computer program to solve a maze of your own creation!

🕐 **TIME FRAME:**
15–30 minutes

MATERIALS

⇨ pencil

⇨ graph paper

⇨ partner

SCIENCE TAKEAWAY

Computers follow programming instructions literally, even if the instructions are wrong. Sometimes you need to run a program and see the errors before you can debug it.

1. Draw a small maze on the graph paper. Each wall should be vertical or horizontal. Label the "start" and "finish" squares.

2. Imagine you are standing on the Start square. On a separate sheet of paper, write directions for walking through the maze to reach the Finish. Use commands such as "Move forward two squares" or "Turn left."

3. Instruct your partner to follow your maze directions exactly, even if there's a mistake.

4. If your partner made it all the way to the Finish, then congratulations! Your program did not have any bugs. In programming, errors are called bugs.

5. If your partner crashed into a wall, debug your program! Carefully review your program step by step to see what went wrong. After you discover the bug, revise your program.

6. Have your partner try the maze again, following your new program. Did it work this time? If not, keep debugging your program until your partner completes the maze.

LED STICKIES

Light up your room with these mini magnetic light-emitting diodes (LEDs). Or clip them to your clothes to make a glowing fashion statement.

🕐 **TIMEFRAME: 10 minutes**

MATERIALS

⇨ assorted LEDs

⇨ size 2032 coin cell batteries

⇨ clear tape

⇨ scissors

⇨ magnetic tape

⇨ magnetic surface (such as a refrigerator or filing cabinet)

SCIENCE TAKEAWAY

LEDs convert electric current into light. They use less energy than other light bulbs, and they don't get as hot. That's why LEDs are commonly used in holiday lights!

1. Each LED has two legs, or leads. One lead is longer than the other. Pinch the leads of the LED around a battery, so one lead touches each side. Make sure the LED's long lead touches the + side of the battery. The LED should light up!

2. Hold the LED's leads in place by wrapping the battery tightly in a piece of clear tape. When you let go, the LED should stay lit.

3. Cut a square piece of magnetic tape about the same size as the battery. Place it on one side of the battery. Then wrap the battery in another piece of clear tape.

4. Place your LED sticky on a magnetic surface. Turn off the lights, or wait until night to see how it looks in the dark. The light in your LED sticky should last for one to two weeks.

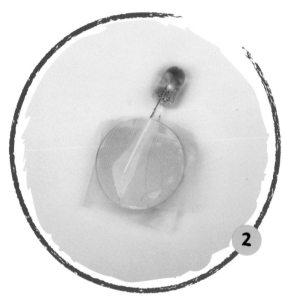

LIGHT-UP PAPER CIRCUIT

Add LEDs to your art projects to give them an extra glow!

🕐 **TIMEFRAME: 15 minutes**

MATERIALS

⇨ scissors

⇨ copper tape

⇨ construction paper

⇨ assorted LEDs

⇨ clear tape

⇨ size 2032 coin cell batteries

⇨ paper clips

⇨ markers, colored pencils, or crayons (optional)

SCIENCE **TAKEAWAY**

A circuit is a closed pathway made of wires that electric current flows through. In this project, the pathways are the copper tape and the LED's leads. A power source, such as the battery, makes the current move in a circuit. When the current reaches the LED, it gives the LED power to light up.

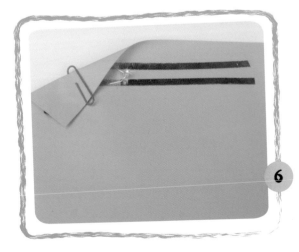

1. Cut two strips of copper tape. Attach the longer strip horizontally about 1 inch (2.5 cm) away from the edge of the paper.

2. Attach the shorter strip about a half inch (1.3 cm) from the longer strip, so the strips are parallel.

3. Each LED has two legs, or leads. Carefully bend the leads. Use clear tape to attach each lead to a strip of copper tape. Put the longer lead on the longer strip of tape and the shorter lead on the shorter strip. Point the LED upward.

4. Place the coin cell battery near the corner of the page on the shorter piece of copper tape. The + symbol on the battery should face up.

5. Fold the corner of the paper so the longer copper strip touches the top of the battery. This should light up your LED.

6. Paper clip the folded paper in place so the LED stays lit. You have made a paper circuit. Want to make an art project? You can poke the LED through the paper so the bulb is on one side and the leads and copper strips are on the other.

7. You can also connect multiple LEDs to one battery. Draw petals around the LEDs to make glowing flowers, or attach LEDs to a holiday card to give it a festive glow!

BRISTLEBOT

Bzz-Bzz! Build your own robot out of a toothbrush head. Watch it buzz across the table, or build two and race them!

🕐 **TIMEFRAME: 20 minutes**

MATERIALS

⇨ toothbrush

⇨ scissors

⇨ pliers

⇨ double-sided foam tape

⇨ wire stripper

⇨ size 2032 coin cell battery with leads

⇨ 3-volt vibration motor with leads

⇨ decorative items such as googly eyes, glitter glue, or pipe cleaners (optional)

SCIENCE TAKEAWAY

You created a circuit between the battery and the motor. The battery was the power source, and it sent electric current through the leads to the motor. When the electric current reached the motor, it powered the motor to make it vibrate.

2

1 With an adult's help, score the toothbrush with scissors. Then use the pliers to break off the handle of the toothbrush.

2 Cut a piece of foam tape the size of the toothbrush head. Stick one side of the tape to one end of the plastic toothbrush head. Press down and hold so the tape is secure.

3 Strip the black and red insulation off the ends of the battery leads. The tips of the leads will be exposed.

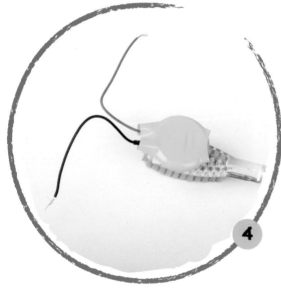

4

4 Attach the flat side of the battery to the other side of the tape. Do not let the leads stick to the tape. Press and hold down to secure the battery. Pull the leads toward the back of the toothbrush head.

5 Attach the motor to the other side of the plastic toothbrush head, so the motor's leads stretch toward the back of the toothbrush head.

6 Twist together the exposed pieces of the red leads. Do the same with the battery's black lead and the motor's blue lead.

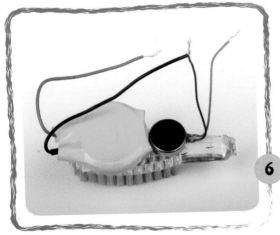

6

7 Your bristlebot should vibrate! Decorate your bristlebot with eyes or whatever you'd like. If your bristlebot stops moving, check the leads. Retwist them if necessary. To turn off your bristlebot, just untwist one set of leads. Turning off your robot will save battery power.

ART BOT

What if you could build a robot that creates its own art? This robot's legs are markers that wobble across a piece of paper, creating a drawing as it moves.

🕐 **TIMEFRAME: 30 minutes**

MATERIALS

⇨ 2 AA batteries

⇨ 2xAA battery holder with on/off switch and leads

⇨ cork

⇨ 3-volt DC motor with leads

⇨ hobby knife

⇨ 16-ounce plastic cup

⇨ double-sided foam tape

⇨ electrical tape

⇨ 3 thin washable markers

⇨ craft stick

⇨ paper

SCIENCE TAKEAWAY

What causes this robot to wobble? The extra weight of the cork and craft stick causes the robot to lean off-center. But it bounces back and forth so quickly that it causes vibrations and the robot moves. Without the off-center weight, the robot wouldn't move at all.

1 Insert the batteries into the battery holder. Press the cork onto the motor shaft.

2 With an adult's help, cut a hole in the bottom center of the plastic cup. Cut two more holes, one to the right and one to the left of the first.

3 Place the cup upside down. Thread the motor leads through the outer holes of the cup. Make sure the motor lines up with the center hole so it can spin freely.

4 Attach double-sided foam tape on either side of the three holes. Press the motor firmly onto the tape. Do not tape the back of the motor shaft.

5 Twist together the exposed metal parts of the motor's red lead and the battery holder's red lead. Do the same with both black leads. Wrap both connections in electrical tape.

6 Tape the battery holder inside the cup. Make sure the power switch is facing toward the rim.

7 Tape the markers to the sides of the cup, to form a tripod. Tape a craft stick along the top of the cork. Remove the marker caps, and place your robot on the paper.

8 Turn the battery holder's power switch on. The craft stick should spin, causing the entire robot to wobble and move around. Replace the paper as needed to create as many pieces of art as you like!

JUNK BOT

Don't throw away your empty bottles or paper towel tubes—turn them into robots!

🕐 **TIMEFRAME: 30 minutes**

MATERIALS

⇨ 2 AA batteries

⇨ 2xAA battery holder with on/off switch and leads

⇨ 3-volt DC motor with leads

⇨ electrical tape

⇨ cork

⇨ recycled materials such as plastic bottles or paper towel tubes

⇨ construction materials (such as craft sticks or straws)

⇨ clear tape, duct tape, rubber bands, zip ties, or glue

⇨ decorative items such as googly eyes, pipe cleaners, construction paper, glitter glue, and crayons and markers

⇨ scissors

SCIENCE TAKEAWAY

Robots can be made from a variety of materials. Using recycled materials helps keep them out of landfills, where the materials may take up to five hundred years to break down. Recycling helps the environment!

1. Insert the AA batteries into the battery holder. Twist together the exposed metal parts of the motor's red lead and the battery holder's red lead. Do the same with both black leads. Wrap both connections in electrical tape.

2. Press the curved side of the cork onto the motor shaft. The cork should be off-center.

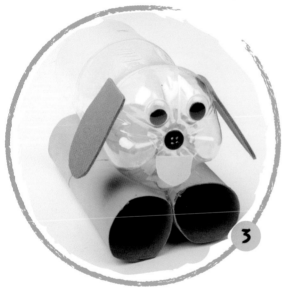

3. Build a body for your robot out of recycled and craft materials such as paper towel tubes, water bottles, and more. There is no wrong way to do this step. What you build is up to you. Don't forget to decorate your robot!

4. Attach the battery holder and motor to your robot's body. But don't glue or tape the battery holder shut or make it difficult to access. (Eventually you will need to replace the batteries.) Make sure that the cork can rotate without getting stuck against the robot's body and that the leads don't get tangled in the cork when the robot moves.

5. Turn your battery holder on, put your robot on the floor, and watch it go!

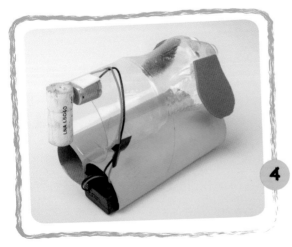

DANCING ROBOT

Have you ever seen a robot dance? Build your own flipping, tumbling robot that can dance around!

TIMEFRAME: 30 minutes

MATERIALS

⇨ 3 AA batteries

⇨ 3xAA battery holder with on/off switch and leads

⇨ 2 corks

⇨ 2 geared 4.5-volt DC motors with leads and breadboard pins

⇨ duct tape

⇨ 2 craft sticks

⇨ scissors

⇨ double-sided foam tape

⇨ hot glue gun

⇨ mini breadboard (also known as a protoboard)

⇨ decorative items such as pipe cleaners or googly eyes (optional)

SCIENCE TAKEAWAY

You added two loads, or items to power, to your circuit. One power source, the battery, powers two motors. This creates a parallel circuit. The electrical current from the battery splits in two and flows to each motor separately.

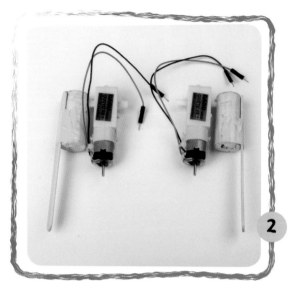

3

2

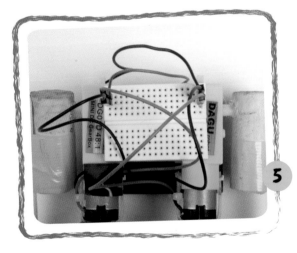

5

1. Insert the batteries into the battery holder. Duct tape a craft stick to each cork.

2. Press one cork onto a motor shaft to create a hole. Remove the cork and fill the hole with hot glue. Press the cork back onto the shaft. Repeat for the second cork and motor.

3. Place double-sided foam tape on the battery holder. Press one side of the motors onto the tape. Point the motors in the same direction. Remove the paper backing from the breadboard, and stick the breadboard onto the top of the motors.

4. The breadboard should be horizontal, so the wider length is going left to right. With an adult's help, plug the battery holder's black lead into the upper-right hole of the breadboard. Plug the battery holder's red lead into the upper left hole of the breadboard.

5. For the first motor, plug the black lead into the breadboard underneath the battery holder's black lead. Plug the red lead underneath the battery holder's red one. For the second motor, plug the red lead underneath the black ones and the black lead underneath the red ones.

6. Switch the power on. The motors should spin, making your robot dance! You can switch the red and black leads for either motor to change the direction the motor spins. This will make your robot dance differently! Give it some personality by decorating it.

UNDERWATER ROBOT

H_2O

Learn how robots and other machines can travel underwater by creating your very own underwater robot!

TIMEFRAME:
Part 1: 15 minutes
Part 2: 30 minutes

MATERIALS

⇨ 3-volt DC motor with leads

⇨ 3 5-gram packs self-setting rubber

⇨ scissors

⇨ heat-shrink tubing in the following sizes: $1/24$ inches (1 mm), $1/12$ inches (2 mm), $1/8$ inches (3 mm), and $1/6$ inches (4 mm)

⇨ hair dryer

⇨ epoxy

⇨ toothpicks

⇨ model boat propeller

⇨ 2 AA batteries

⇨ 22-gauge insulated hook-up wire, stranded black

⇨ 22-gauge insulated hook-up wire, stranded red

⇨ 2xAA battery holder with on/off switch and leads

⇨ wire stripper

⇨ electrical tape

⇨ 2 film canisters with caps

⇨ duct tape

⇨ child-sized plastic clothes hanger

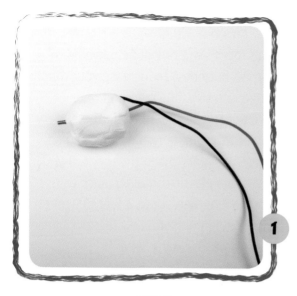

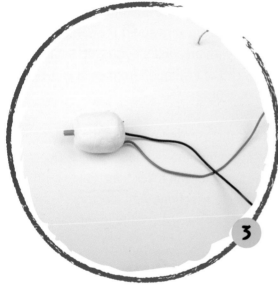

PART 1

1. Cover the motor in self-setting rubber to create a waterproof shell. Let the two leads and the motor's shaft stick out from the rubber.

2. Cut several segments of the heat-shrink tubing at about the same length as the motor's shaft.

3. Slip a $1/24$-inch (1 mm) segment of tubing onto the motor's shaft. Use a hair dryer to shrink-fit the tubing onto the shaft. Repeat with the other pieces of tubing, increasing in diameter. Repeat until the outer diameter of the tubing is about the same size as the inner diameter of the propeller.

4. Follow the instructions on the container to mix the epoxy. Using a toothpick, place a small amount of epoxy inside the propeller's cylinder. Carefully insert the motor's shaft into the propeller. Be careful not to let any epoxy go all the way down to the base of the motor's shaft, as this could prevent it from spinning. Once the propeller is pressed all the way onto the shaft, apply a dab of epoxy to the other end to help seal it in place.

5. Put your motor in a safe place until tomorrow. The self-setting rubber and epoxy both take twenty-four hours to harden completely.

PART 2

1. Your robot's motor will be powered by two AA batteries. To increase your robot's range, use two long pieces of hookup wire to connect the motor to the battery holder. The wire length will depend on where you plan to test the robot. If you test it in a plastic container, such as a storage bin, then about 3 feet (0.9 m) of wire should do. If you test the robot in a larger area, use more wire.

2. Use the wire strippers to cut one piece of red hookup wire and one piece of black hookup wire about the same length. Then, with an adult's help, strip a half inch (1.3 cm) of insulation from each end of each wire.

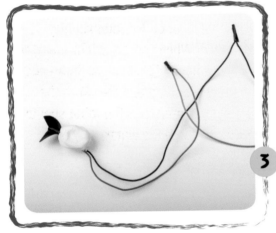

3. Twist the exposed pieces of the motor's red lead and the red hookup wire. Do the same for the black lead. Cover both connected sections with electrical tape. Make sure there are no holes or gaps in the tape.

4. Repeat step 3 to connect the other ends of the hookup wires to the battery holder. Insert the AA batteries into the battery holder.

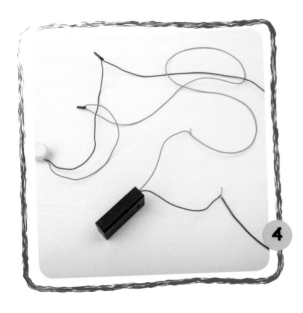

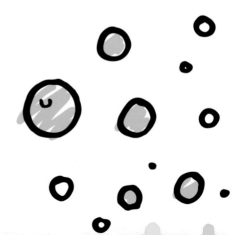

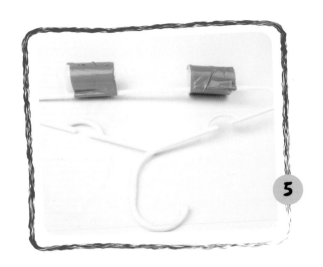

5. Tightly secure the lids on the film canisters. Then use duct tape to attach them to the longest edge of the clothes hanger.

6. Twist together the two red hookup wires and the two black hookup wires. Wrap the connections in electrical tape. Use electrical tape to hold both sets of wires together along their length.

7. Duct tape the waterproofed motor to the hanger's hook. Give the propeller room to rotate freely. Do not let it touch the hanger or get stuck in the duct tape.

8. Take your robot on an underwater adventure! When you place it in the water, lower the hook of the hanger first. Keep the battery out of the water. Turn the battery holder on, and the robot should move down into the water.

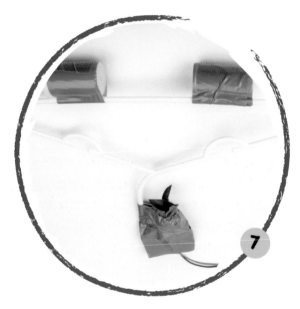

SCIENCE TAKEAWAY

Your robot's film canisters give it buoyancy so it can float. When the propeller spins, it pushes on the water, and the water pushes back on the robot. This lets the robot overcome its buoyancy and dive down into the water.

ROBOT HAND

Have you ever wondered how your hand works? This robot will teach you! Build a robot modeled after the human hand, and see what you can grab!

 TIMEFRAME:
Part 1: 10 minutes
Part 2: 20 minutes

MATERIALS

⇒ 5 disposable drinking straws (straws that pop back into shape when squeezed)

⇒ cutting board

⇒ scissors

⇒ ruler

⇒ permanent marker

⇒ dental floss

⇒ sewing needles (eyes of the needle as small as possible but fitting the dental floss; longer needles preferred)

⇒ needle-nose pliers, chopsticks, or beading pliers

⇒ at least 15 rubber washers

⇒ 1 piece of thick cardboard

⇒ superglue

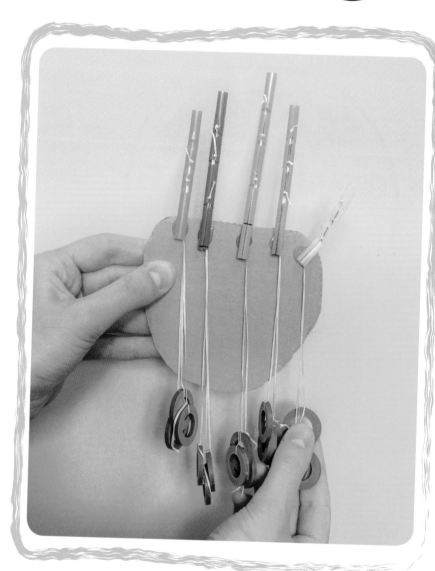

PART 1

1 Your robot hand needs joints, or points where the fingers can bend. If your straw doesn't have a line down its length, draw one. Select one end of the straw to be a fingertip. At the other end, mark where you want the finger to end, but don't cut it yet.

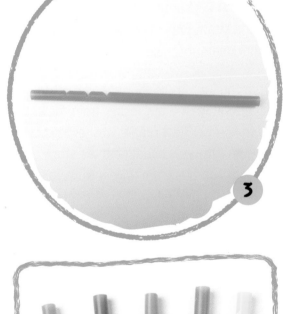

2 Most fingers have three sections, but you can choose how many sections your robot hand's fingers will have. Look at your own hand for inspiration! Make a mark along the straw's line where you want each joint to go.

3 Place a straw flat on your work surface with the line facing up. With an adult's help, cut notches into each mark along the straw's line. Then try bending all the joints at the same time. The straw should gently form a nice curve if you lined up all the cuts along the straight line you drew.

4 Repeat steps 1 through 3 to create the rest of your robot hand's fingers. If you want the hand to have a thumb, cut that straw slightly shorter.

PART 2

1 Cut one of the straw fingers to the length you want it. Make sure to leave some extra length of straw so you can attach it to the palm of your robot hand.

2 Cut a piece of thread at least four times the length of the finger. Near one end of the thread, tie a big knot. With an adult's help, thread the other end through the needle.

3 Carefully poke the needle through the straw just above the top joint. Using pliers, pass the needle down the length of the straw until it comes out the opposite end of the straw. Repeat with threads on the other joints.

4 Trim the threads so they are all the same length, at least a few inches from the end of the straw. Tie a rubber washer to each thread. With one hand, hold the straw upright and place the fingers from your other hand through the rings. Gently pull the rings one at a time, and watch the finger bend!

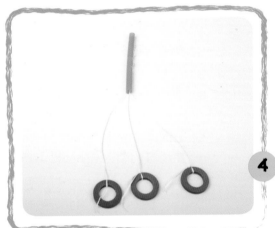

SCIENCE TAKEAWAY

Your hands are made of bones, tendons, and muscles. The bones are connected by joints just like the notches in your straws. The muscles pull on the tendons, which act like your strings, causing the joints to bend.

5

5 Repeat steps 1 through 4 to complete the rest of the fingers for your robot hand.

6 To create the palm of your robot hand, cut the cardboard the size and shape you'd like the palm to be. With an adult's help, glue the bottom ends of the finger straws to the cardboard palm. Look at where your fingers are placed on your own hand, and try to place the fingers in a similar way on the cardboard palm.

6

7 Your robot hand is complete! Tug on the rings to make one finger move, or tug on all of them to close your robot hand into a fist. Practice grasping and holding different objects. If your hand doesn't work exactly the way you'd like it to, try again!

WRAPPING UP

After you've completed your awesome robotics projects, make sure to clean up! Put away all materials, throw away garbage, and clean off your workspace. Store your robotics projects in a safe place so they won't get damaged.

Continue exploring the world of science and technology. What did you learn while working on these projects? Try the same project, but do something differently next time! If something didn't work the first time around, think about what changes you can make, and do it again. You can do a lot with robotics. Keep experimenting!

For more information on materials kits and even more free robotics projects, scan this QR code!

INDEX

PHOTO ACKNOWLEDGMENTS

The images in this book are used with the permission of: Design element (pencil) © primiaou/Shutterstock Images, pp. 8, 10, 12, 14, 16, 18, 20, 25, 28; © Visual Generation/Shutterstock Images, pp. 1 (clock), 30 (clock); © Sashatigar/Shutterstock Images, pp. 1 (robot head), 3 (lightning bolt, atom), 14 (robot head), 20 (lightning bolt), 29 (robot); © primiaou/Shutterstock Images, pp. 1 (magnet), 9 (maze), 11 (magnet); © Tiwat K/Shutterstock Images, pp. 1 (angle), 16 (paint pallet), 19 (recycling arrow), 22 (H2O), 31 (computer); © Steve Debenport/iStockphoto, pp. 4 (girl with wires), 6 (teacher and students); © Mighty Media, Inc., pp. 5-29 (project photos), 7 (battery pack, moldable glue, copper tape, wire stripper, motor, pliers), 10 (LED lights), 12 (LED lights), 26 (hand); © DariaRoozen/Shutterstock Images, p. 9 (question mark); © VectorShow/Shutterstock Images, p. 18 (water bottle); © Artur Balytskyi/Shutterstock Images, p. 24 (bubbles)

Front cover: © primiaou/Shutterstock Images (light bulb, magnet, square); © Sashatigar/Shutterstock Images (robot head); © STILLFX/Shutterstock Images (background); © Visual Generation/Shutterstock Images (clock)

Back cover: © DariaRoozen/Shutterstock Images (question marks); © primiaou/Shutterstock Images (pencil); © Sashatigar/Shutterstock Images (LED lights, lightning bolts); © STILLFX/Shutterstock Images (background)

GLOSSARY

buoyancy: the tendency of an object to float or rise when in a liquid

circuit: a complete path electricity travels through to provide power to an object

debug: to get rid of errors in a computer program

diameter: the distance measured across the center of a circle

electric current: the flow of electric charge in a circuit

exposed: uncovered and open to view

lead: the wire or metal leg used to attach an electrical part to a circuit

load: an item being powered by a circuit

parallel circuit: a circuit in which electrical current splits into multiple paths

power source: the object, usually a battery, that provides electricity in a circuit

programming: creating a set of instructions and actions for a computer

score: to mark the surface of something with marks, lines, or scratches

tripod: something that rests on three legs

FURTHER INFORMATION

For more information and projects, visit **Science Buddies** at
https://www.sciencebuddies.org/.

Hustad, Douglas. *Discover Robotics.* Minneapolis: Lerner Publications, 2017.

Ives, Rob. *Build Your Own Robots.* Minneapolis: Hungry Tomato, 2018.

Murphy, Maggie. *High-Tech DIY Projects with Robotics.* New York: PowerKids, 2015.